FUN-FILLED 5- to 10-MINUTE SOCIAL STUDIES ACTIVITIES FOR YOUNG LEARNERS

200 Instant Kid-Pleasing Activities That Build Early Social Studies Skills for Circle Time, Transition Time—or Any Time!

by Deborah Diffily and Charlotte Sassman

SCHOLASTIC PROFESSIONAL BOOKS

NEW YORK   TORONTO   LONDON   AUCKLAND   SYDNEY
MEXICO CITY   NEW DELHI   HONG KONG   BUENOS AIRES

Cover design by Josué Castilleja
Illustrations by Cary Pillo

ISBN 0-439-42054-7

1 2 3 4 5 6 7 8 9 10   40   09 08 07 06 05 04 03

TABLE OF CONTENTS

ABOUT THIS BOOK

Early childhood educators acknowledge an old teaching adage: There is never enough time during the day to teach everything that needs to be taught. All too often, social studies is neglected because state and local mandates emphasize reading and math instruction.

Beginning with the beliefs of Thomas Jefferson, social studies has long been valued for helping create an educated population. A clear understanding of social-studies concepts is necessary in order to be an active citizen within a democracy. The National Council for Social Studies (NCSS), the leading professional organization for social studies, asserts, "The primary purpose of social studies is to help young people develop the ability to make informed and reasoned decisions for the public good as citizens of a culturally diverse, democratic society in an interdependent world."

With such important goals at stake, teachers of young children search for ways to ensure that social-studies concepts are taught. This book offers one solution to the quest for more time to teach social studies: involving young children in brief activities related to social studies that lead them into deeper understandings about democracy, diverse cultures, and more.

The learning experiences in this book are organized around the 10 themes established in 1994 by NCSS in their curriculum-standards document, *Expectations for Excellence*. This book introduces each theme and puts the learning experiences into the context of the social-studies standards. These themes are:

1. Culture
During the early years of school, exploring the concepts of similarities and differences makes the study of culture appropriate. Socially, young learners are beginning to interact with other students, some of whom are like them and some of whom are different.

2. Time, Continuity, and Change

Young learners establish a sense of order and time through sequencing. They enjoy hearing stories of the recent past and of long ago. In addition, they begin to recognize that individuals may hold different views about the past, and to understand the link between human decisions and consequences.

3. People, Places, and Environment

In the early grades, children draw upon immediate personal experiences as a basis for exploring geographic concepts and skills. They also express interest in distant and unfamiliar things, and are concerned about the use and abuse of the physical environment.

4. Individual Development and Identity

Observing brothers and sisters, looking at family photo albums, and remembering past achievements and anticipating the future are examples of how young learners can develop their personal identities in the context of families, peers, schools, and communities.

5. Individuals, Groups, and Institutions

Young children should have opportunities to examine various institutions that affect their lives and influence their thinking. They should also explore ways in which institutions, such as churches or health-care networks, are created to respond to changing individual and group needs.

6. Power, Authority, and Governance

Learners in the early grades explore their natural and developing sense of fairness and order as they experience relationships with others. They develop an increasingly comprehensive awareness of rights and responsibilities in specific contexts.

7. Production, Distribution, and Consumption

Children need to differentiate between wants and needs. They explore economic decisions as they compare their own economic experiences with those of others and consider the wider consequences of those decisions on groups, communities, the nation, and beyond.

8. Science, Technology, and Society

Young children can learn how their daily lives are intertwined with technology. They can study how basic technologies have evolved and how we have employed technology to modify our physical environment. They can construct examples of how technologies altered the course of history.

9. Global Connections

Through exposure to various media and firsthand experiences, young learners become aware of and are affected by events on a global scale. Within this context, children examine and explore global connections and basic issues and concerns, suggesting and initiating responsive action plans.

10. Civic Ideals and Practices

Activities such as helping to set classroom expectations, examining experiences in relation to ideals, and determining how to balance the needs of individuals and the group serve as an introduction to civic ideals and practices. Stories and drama also offer views of citizenship in other times and places.

Note that some of the activities in this book may take more than 5 to 10 minutes, while some may take less. For example, a few activities call for grandparents to come in and talk with children about the "old days." While grandparents may visit the classroom for several hours, the formal interaction between grandparents and children lasts only about 10 minutes. Other activities may take only a moment, but are repeated throughout the day. Some activities are short individual lessons planned for several days in a row, while other activities are introduced to the whole group then completed during independent study or center time.

Rather than selecting an activity for the amount of time it takes, choose an activity because of how it pertains to the class's learning. Keep in mind young children's limited attention span and vary learning activities accordingly.

Enjoy the book!

CULTURE

W Whole-group activity   **S** Small-group activity

I Individual activity   **T** Transition   **RA** Read-aloud

W We Are All Alike

Ask children to brainstorm how everyone in the class is the same. Young children will probably need prompting, with comments such as, *"Let's think. Does everybody in our class eat food? Does everyone wear shirts or blouses? Does everyone wear shoes?"*

RA *All Kinds of Children*
by Norma Simon (Albert Whitman, 1999)

Watercolor illustrations in this book lead the reader through a discussion of things children around the world have in common: food, clothing, love, an opportunity to play, and even a belly button.

W We All Eat Bread

Bring different kinds of bread to class (or ask families to share their favorite kind of bread) and have a bread-tasting session. (Make sure to check for food allergies first.)

Read Ann Morris's *Bread, Bread, Bread* (Scott Foresman, 1993) as an introduction to this activity.

W Fruit Salad

Ask each family to send in a piece of fruit that is common to their country of heritage. Write a repetitive poem on chart paper, such as:

> **Breanna brought plantains.**
> **She eats them at home.**
> **Wesley and Christi brought apples.**
> **They eat them at home.**
> **John brought blueberries.**
> **He eats them at home.**

After chanting the poem a couple of times and pointing out the repetitive words (*brought, eat, them, at, home*) distribute a paper plate and plastic knife to each child. Ask them to cut up their piece of fruit and add all the pieces to a large bowl. Then offer fruit salad for snack. (Make sure to check for food allergies first.)

W Shoe Collection

Ask children to bring different kinds of shoes to class. Contact international students at a local university to add to the collection. Discuss why certain shoes are worn at specific times.

RA *Hats, Hats, Hats*
by Ann Morris (Mulberry, 1993)

Morris's beautiful photographs show hats from cultures around the world.

Try This! Set up a learning center with newspaper, construction paper, card stock, sentence strips, markers, and all kinds of collage materials. Invite children to design and create their own hats.

W Holidays Around Our Class

Ask the families in your class to briefly write about a family tradition related to a holiday. Read and discuss one family's tradition with the class each day. Point out that everyone celebrates holidays in their own ways and it is these differences that make each celebration special. Extend this activity to include not only the more predictable winter holidays (Christmas, Hanukkah, Kwanzaa) but also Memorial Day, Fourth of July, Halloween, or Labor Day.

W Our International Holidays

Ask families to share celebrations that are related to their heritage. For example, Japanese people celebrate a special Children's Day, Hispanic people celebrate Cinco de Mayo, and people of Chinese descent celebrate Chinese New Year.

Teaching Tip

In celebrating other cultures' holidays, avoid a "tourist" curriculum by including several other aspects of cultures too. For example, don't just eat tacos and dance the Mexican Hat Dance on May 5. Throughout the year, read books and poetry, examine art, and listen to the music of various cultures.

W Mexico and Canada

While learning about our neighbors to the north and south, post a large map of North America. As children learn facts about Mexico or Canada, post each fact on the map near the country. This will reinforce the similarities and differences between the countries. Extend the activity by creating a Venn diagram to illustrate how Canada, Mexico, and the United States are alike and different.

(T) I Say "Hello"

To the tune of "Farmer in the Dell," sing:

> I say hello,
> I say hello,
> Every time I see someone,
> I say hello.

Substitute words for *hello* from other languages, such as *hola* in Spanish, *hei* in Norwegian, *bonjour* in French, *ciao* in Italian, or *hallo* in German. Help children understand that even though people use different words, every culture uses a greeting.

(RA) *Mothers, Fathers, Sisters, and Brothers: A Collection of Family Poems*
by Mary Ann Hoberman (Little, Brown, 2001)

This collection of poems illustrates a variety of family situations. All children will relate to these poems in one way or another.

(RA) *Brothers & Sisters*
by Ellen B. Senisi (Scholastic, 2001)

Using little text (mostly captions for culturally sensitive photographs), this book's unifying theme comes from the photos themselves. Each photograph shows an older sibling with a younger one, celebrating the sibling relationship.

Try This! Ask children to identify ways in which they are like the children in the book. Then guide children to pretend to be a character in the book while expressing worries or problems. Quick dramatizations of these scenarios can be fun and can also help young children understand that not all sibling relationships are exactly like their own.

(RA) The Shaman's Apprentice: A Tale of the Amazon Rain Forest
by Lynne Cherry and Mark J. Plotkin (Gulliver, 1998)

This book shows the life of Kamanyu, who dreams of being the next medicine man for his village. Both the text and illustrations show life in a remote village in the Amazon rain forest.

(RA) Midnight: A Cinderella Alphabet
by Stephanie Perkal (Shen's Books, 1997)

A grandmother shares stories of Cinderella with her two grandchildren. Using letters of the alphabet to organize the book, Perkal shares 21 Cinderella stories from 18 cultures. This book reinforces the fact that no matter how different another culture may seem, all people have many things in common.

Try This! Collect versions of Cinderella from different cultures. Read one a day and talk about what each tale shows about the culture it represents.

(RA) Jingle Dancer
by Cynthia Leitich Smith (HarperCollins, 1999)

In this non-stereotypical portrayal of Native American life, Jenna gets support from friends and family as she prepares for the big dance at an upcoming powwow. The focus of the story is Jenna's love for jingle dancing and how she prepares her jingle dress.

Try This! Locate an audiotape or CD of authentic Native American music that might be played at a powwow. Introduce the repetitive steps of many Native American dances and encourage children to join you in dancing to the rhythm of the music.

RA My Father's Boat

by Sherry Garland (Scholastic, 1998)

Garland tells the story of a father who takes his son fishing in the Pacific Ocean, just off the coast of California. During their fishing trip, the father talks about their Vietnamese heritage, culture, and values.

Try This! Invite someone from the local community who is knowledgeable about his or her own Vietnamese heritage to talk to the class about Vietnamese culture.

RA An Amish Year

by Richard Ammon (Atheneum, 2000)

This book is just what the title implies—the story of a traditional Amish family's life over an entire year.

Try This! Use a Venn diagram to help children organize the parts of their lives that are different from the Amish, parts of the Amish life that are different from their lives, and the things they have in common.

TIME, CONTINUITY, AND CHANGE

W Whole-group activity   **S** Small-group activity
I Individual activity   **T** Transition   **RA** Read-aloud

W Family Share Time

Invite families to come to the class and share something from their past. Suggest topics such as communication, music, clothing, or anything else that changes from generation to generation. For example, a mother might visit wearing bell-bottom jeans, love beads, and a headband and playing a Beatles' song, or a grandfather might wear a zoot suit and talk about how long it took for a letter to get to different parts of the country (compared to today's instant e-mail) or how long it took to travel to a distant city (compared to today's supersonic jets).

W Dressing Up for the Decade

Over several days or weeks, ask a family member to come to class dressed in clothing that represents different decades (1990s, 1980s, 1970s, and so on) and play a song or two from that decade. Photograph each family's share time and post the photos on a time line.

W Farms Past and Present

Locate two different farmers in your community: one who lived on a small family farm in the early to mid-1900s, and one who lives on a large working farm today. Ask the two guests to talk about their farms and how farming has changed.

RA *Century Farm: One Hundred Years on a Family Farm*
by Alvis Upitis (Boyd Mills, 2000)

Photographs of one farm and the family who works on it support this story of a Wisconsin farm. The story begins 100 years ago and ends in the present day. Differences and similarities in farming over the years are made clear.

W Grandparents' Day

Declare a particular day as Grandparents' Day. Invite children's grandparents to visit the class on that day and join the class in regular activities. Throughout the day, take breaks from the regular schedule to let one grandparent share stories of his or her youth. While some grandparents might spend an hour or more with the class, limit the time they share to ten minutes or so. This schedule gives each visitor an opportunity to speak to the whole group without pushing the limits of young children's attention spans. Also, it offers the grandparents some time for informal conversations with the children, especially those who may not interact with older adults on a regular basis.

RA Literacy Links

Throughout the weeks before and after Grandparents' Day, read books that focus on the lives of children's grandparents. Here are some suggestions:

- *Halmoni's Day* by Edna Coe Bercaw (Puffin, 2000)
  This is the story of Jennifer's grandmother, who travels all the way from Korea to attend Grandparents' Day at Jennifer's school.

- *Grandaddy's Street Songs* by Monalisa DeGross (Sun/Hyperion, 2000)
  A grandfather describes one day when he was a young man working as a street vendor, selling produce from his wagon.

- *Grandfather's Work: A Traditional Healer in Nigeria* by Ifeoma Onyefulu (Millbrook, 1998)
  A child describes his grandfather's work as a traditional healer in a Nigerian village.

Teaching Tip
Let your school librarian know that you are looking for books for the above activity, and ask him or her to order as many books as the budget allows. You can also make friends with the children's librarian at the local public library and ask that you be notified when books of certain types you need come into the library.

W Trees That Change

Early in the school year, note the appearance of a large tree on the school grounds or in the neighborhood. As the year progresses and the seasons change, note the changes in the tree. Invite children to draw an illustration of the tree for each season, and label each picture with the name of the season.

W Daily Schedule

To reinforce the concept of sequence, post the day's schedule in a pocket chart. As you go through the day, turn each card over as that part of the schedule is completed. Use transition words such as *next*, *after that*, *last*, and *before* as you discuss the schedule.

1 Morning, Afternoon, and Night

Give each child a large piece of paper folded into three parts. Ask children to label the parts *morning*, *afternoon*, and *night*. Encourage them to draw or write about what they do during each of these times. As children share their work, point out how many people do the same thing at the same time but perhaps in a different way.

RA *Annushka's Voyage*
by Edith Tarbescu (Clarion, 1998)

Anya and her little sister Tanya endure rough travel to America on a steamship, passing through Ellis Island, then meeting their father in New York City.

RA *Squanto's Journey: The Story of the First Thanksgiving*
by Joseph Bruchac (Silver Whistle, 2000)

This tells more of the story of Squanto than children typically hear. Squanto was taken captive and sold in Spain as a slave. Freed by monks, he was allowed to return to America. Much later, he met the English people who arrived on the *Mayflower*, and offered help during their first hard winter. With historic accuracy and detailed illustrations, *Squanto's Journey* offers a rich account of the first Thanksgiving.

PEOPLE, PLACES, AND ENVIRONMENT

W Whole-group activity   **S** Small-group activity

I Individual activity   **T** Transition   **RA** Read-aloud

W Wants and Needs

Before school, hang a large piece of craft paper on a bulletin board. Divide it in half, and label one side *Wants* and the other side *Needs*. Talk to children about the difference between the things we want and the things we need. Then have children dictate things they have at home, and write

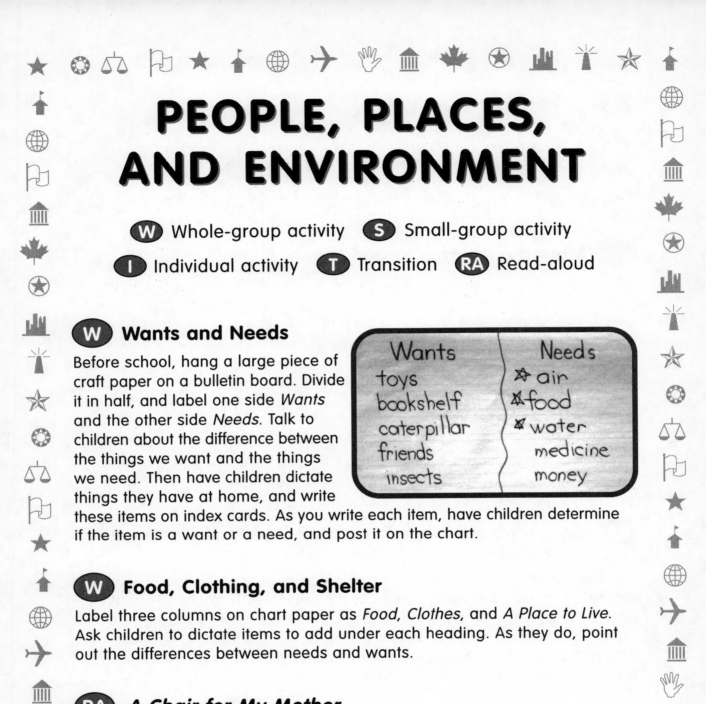

Wants	Needs
toys	air
bookshelf	food
caterpillar	water
friends	medicine
insects	money

these items on index cards. As you write each item, have children determine if the item is a want or a need, and post it on the chart.

W Food, Clothing, and Shelter

Label three columns on chart paper as *Food*, *Clothes*, and *A Place to Live*. Ask children to dictate items to add under each heading. As they do, point out the differences between needs and wants.

RA *A Chair for My Mother*
by Vera B. Williams (Scott Foresman, 1984)

After all their furniture is destroyed in a fire, a little girl, her waitress mother, and her grandmother all save coins in a jar. They save enough money to buy a big comfortable chair for their living room.

Try This! Suggest that the class follow the example of the family in *A Chair for My Mother* and save coins in a jar for something the class wants to purchase.

(W) Continent Facts

As a part of the morning routine, present a fact about one of the continents. For example, *"Africa is the warmest continent"* or *"Asia is the largest continent."* Write the fact on an index card and post it on a map near that continent.

(W) I Have a Job

Play the "I Have a Job" riddle game: Begin the game by saying a simple riddle, such as, *"I have a job. I protect people and help them follow traffic rules. I keep people safe. What job do I have?"* The child who gives the correct answer can present the next riddle to the class. List the different jobs on the board.

(W) Left and Right

Choose a child to cover his or her eyes or leave the classroom while you hide an object in the room. As the child searches for the object, encourage other children to give clues by saying *left* or *right* as the child moves toward the object. Offer other clue words for children to use, such as *near* and *far*. Have children take turns hunting for the hidden object.

(W) Taking Care of School Property

Show children two objects (such as teddy bears, tools, quilts, or toy cars)— one new and one old. Discuss the similarities and differences between the two. Introduce the words *repair, maintenance, prevention,* and *care.* Explain that the school property needs care, just like these objects need care.

(W) Blueprint of the Classroom

Before class begins, use a blue felt-tip marker to draw a floor plan of the classroom on chart paper, showing the location of doors, windows, and other built-in features. Create cutout construction-paper shapes to indicate other features in the classroom, such as tables, chairs, bookshelves, and desks. Explain that architects use blueprints such as this when planning a building, then use double-sided tape to add the features to the blueprint.

W Who's Who in Our School?

Collect articles of clothing or props that represent the people who perform various jobs at your school. For example, use a large cooking spoon to represent cafeteria workers, a pencil or telephone for the secretary, a broom and mop for the custodian, and a whistle for the gym teacher. Invite a child to choose a prop and pantomime the job of that worker. Have other children try to guess the job and tell where in the school the worker performs the job.

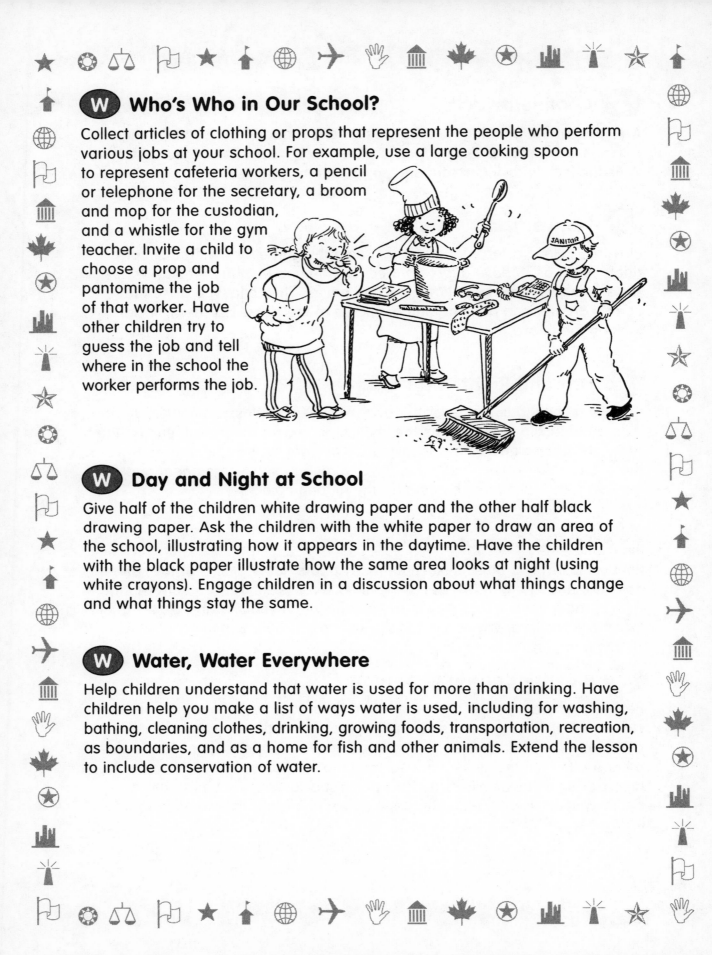

W Day and Night at School

Give half of the children white drawing paper and the other half black drawing paper. Ask the children with the white paper to draw an area of the school, illustrating how it appears in the daytime. Have the children with the black paper illustrate how the same area looks at night (using white crayons). Engage children in a discussion about what things change and what things stay the same.

W Water, Water Everywhere

Help children understand that water is used for more than drinking. Have children help you make a list of ways water is used, including for washing, bathing, cleaning clothes, drinking, growing foods, transportation, recreation, as boundaries, and as a home for fish and other animals. Extend the lesson to include conservation of water.

(S) All the News That's Worth Printing

Buy several different newspapers at a local newsstand or ask friends who live in different towns to send you one of their local newspapers. Divide the class into small groups and ask each group to look at and compare two of the newspapers. Later in the day, come back together as a group to discuss differences in the news that was covered.

(S) Land and Water

Write geographical words such as *plain, hill, mountain, lake, river,* and *ocean* on index cards. Ask small groups of children to sort the cards into two groups: land and water.

(S) Pebbles, Rocks, and Gravel

Add some fist-sized rocks, gravel, and pebbles to the sand table. Encourage children to build paths, walkways, or flower beds, or to simply create patterns in the sand. Small twigs can be added, too.

(I) Summer vs. Winter

At the beginning of a week, lead a discussion about how children dress in the summer and what kinds of activities they do in the summer. Take dictation as children discuss how the summer weather affects what they do. The following day, ask students to draw a picture of themselves during the summer.

The next day, discuss how they dress in the winter and the kinds of activities they do in the winter. Take dictation as children discuss how the winter weather affects what they do. The following day, ask students to draw a picture of themselves during the winter.

On Friday, challenge students to imagine what it must be like to live in climates where it feels like summer all year long or like winter all year long.

(T) This Land Is My Land

Teach students the Woody Guthrie song "This Land Is Your Land." Point out the places mentioned in the song, then use the song as a transition from one activity to another.

(T) Litter in the Classroom

When it's cleanup time, encourage children to pick up scraps of paper by saying, *"Litter bugs beware! We are cleaning up everywhere!"*

Teaching Tip

To extend the experience of cleaning up litter in the classroom, have children put white paper in a recycling bin, pieces of colored paper in a special basket for collage materials, and only throw away paper that cannot be recycled.

(RA) *Miss Rumphius*

by Barbara Cooney (Scott Foresman, 1985)

Miss Rumphius is an elderly woman who remembers that when she was a girl, her grandfather told her to make the world a more beautiful place. Not until she is very old does she figure out what she will do. She thinks of how flowers have always made her life better, and decides to scatter lupine seeds everywhere she goes.

(RA) *Houses and Homes*

by Ann Morris (Lothrop, Lee & Sheppard, 1992)

The color photographs in this book offer a wide view of houses around the world. Different types of building materials, various sizes, and diverse types of homes are noted.

Try This! Display photographs of different kinds of houses around the world (*National Geographic* magazines are a good source for these pictures). Divide the class into small groups. Give each group a picture and ask them to discuss what life might be like in that area, describing the weather, clothing, food, and environment. As each group reports back to the whole group, correct any misconceptions they may have.

RA *A House Is a House for Me*

by Mary Ann Hoberman (Scott Foresman, 1983)

Supported by a text filled with rhyme and rhythm, this book depicts all kinds of houses for people and animals alike.

Try This! Use the detailed illustrations in Hoberman's book to challenge young children to draw detailed pictures of their own houses. Bind the individual pages together into a class book, titled "Houses Are Houses for Us."

RA *Mapping Penny's World*

by Loreen Leedy (Holt, 2000)

Lisa learns about maps at school, then begins making all kinds of maps—of her bedroom, of the trails she rides her bike on, even of the places her dog hides his toys.

Try This! Challenge children to draw a map of the classroom or one of the rooms in their house.

INDIVIDUAL DEVELOPMENT AND IDENTITY

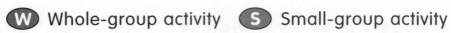

W Whole-group activity   **S** Small-group activity

I Individual activity   **T** Transition   **RA** Read-aloud

W Alike and Different

Gather children in the meeting area. Select three or four children with a particular attribute in common—such as long hair, blue pants, shoes that tie, or a short-sleeved shirt—and ask them to stand. Challenge the other children to discover what is alike about this small group. Point out how the children are both alike and different.

RA *A to Z: Do You Ever Feel Like Me?*
by Bonnie Hausman (Dutton/Penguin Putnam, 1999)

Photographs of children in this book show different feelings, from A to Z. The margins of each page depict cultural objects that begin with the letter on that page.

RA *The Colors of Us*
by Karen Katz (Henry Holt, 1999)

This story follows Lena and her mother as they observe how differences in skin color match the color of foods and things found in nature.

Try This! Use *A to Z: Do You Ever Feel Like Me?* and *The Colors of Us* to spark conversations about how we are the same and how we are different.

S Friends Help Each Other

Divide the class into small groups. Ask each group to talk about specific things they do to help their friends, then work together to create a mural of children helping each other.

S Adults Help Each Other

As a comparison, ask families to allow their children to interview them about specific things they do as adults to help their friends. Ask children to share findings from family interviews and create a mural of adults helping each other.

Teaching Tip
Sometimes young children have difficulty recalling times that they help each other. For several days before you plan to do this activity, point out their helping actions to children.

I When I Get Bigger

Challenge children to imagine themselves as they become adults. Have them complete this sentence starter: *"When I get bigger, I am going to...."* Invite children to draw a picture of themselves as adults. The following day, encourage them to share their drawings.

The Things I Want

Have children think about one item that they wish they could have, then write or draw about how they could go about getting that item.

    The next day, repeat the activity, except have children think about an item they think their parents wish they could have.

    On the third day, have a conversation about the differences in how children and adults get things they want. Discuss children's dependency on adults for money.

Everyone Grows

Ask children to talk with their families about what they were like when they were infants, toddlers, preschoolers, and their current age, using "This Is Me..." (page 29) as a guide.

    On Monday, invite children to draw or write about themselves as babies. On Tuesday, ask them to draw or write about themselves as toddlers. On Wednesday, have children draw or write about themselves as preschoolers. On Thursday, ask children to draw or write about themselves as they are now. On Friday, encourage children to share their work with a partner.

> **Teaching Tip**
> Any time you want young children to discuss a specific topic with their families, send a note home explaining the children's assignment and encouraging families' participation. Young children have the best of intentions, but many will have forgotten what you've asked them to do by the time they are home with their families in the evening.

When My Parents Were Little

Ask students to talk with their parents about how their lives were different as children. Send home copies of "When My _____ Was Little,..." (page 30) and ask families to help their child finish this sentence: "*When my _____ was little,...*" Combine all the pages into a class book and read it to the whole group.

Teaching Tip

For young children, understanding the past begins with remembering their own personal experiences when they were little. Then they move to thinking about when their parents were children and when their grandparents were children. Activities such as interviewing family members, making a family scrapbook, and putting family photographs in chronological order help young children begin to understand the concept of history. Sharing this information with families and encouraging them to make time for some of these activities will benefit their children.

I Preferences

Distribute clipboards, pencils, and copies of "Do You Like..." (page 31) to children. Ask children to think of two foods that are sort of alike (for example, apples and oranges, hamburgers and hot dogs, corn chips and potato chips) and write these words at the top of the page. Have each child interview up to six classmates to figure out which of the two foods their classmates prefer. Then invite children to come back together in a group to talk about how people prefer different foods. Introduce the word *preference*.

RA *Uptown*
by Bryan Collier (Holt, 2000)

Collier's beautiful illustrations in watercolor and collage depict the high points of the Harlem neighborhood in New York, including the Apollo Theater, brownstone row houses, and local chicken and waffle shops. A young boy leads the book's tour of the neighborhood.

Try This! Set up a learning center with the book *Uptown*, and some watercolors and collage materials. As children choose this center, ask them to create a page with illustrations and text to show either their own neighborhood or the school's neighborhood.

RA Best Friends
by Loretta Krupinski (Hyperion, 1998)

Set in the 1870s, this is the story of a friendship that develops between Charlotte, who moves from Kansas to Idaho, and Lily, a Nez Perce girl who already lives in the Snake River Valley.

RA Let's Talk About It: Extraordinary Friends
by Fred Rogers (Putnam, 1999)

Mister Rogers, in his gentle way, talks frankly about children with special needs, and helps children understand that not everybody develops in the same ways.

RA Just Kids: Visiting a Class for Children With Special Needs
by Ellen B. Senisi (Dutton, 1998)

Using photographs to support reader's understanding, this is the story of a girl named Cindy, who carelessly makes a cruel remark. Because of this, Cindy must spend some time every day in a classroom for children with special needs. She soon makes friends with the children in the classroom and learns to appreciate their unique qualities.

This Is Me...

...as a Baby	...as a Toddler
...as a Preschooler	**...Now**

Name_____ **Date**_____

Families: Your child is learning about how people grow and change. Please help your child complete the sentence, describing something that happened to you when you were little. For example, your child might write: *"When my mom was little, she lived in Texas."* Encourage your child to explain incidents from mom's early life.

When My _____ Was Little,...

_____

_____

_____

_____

_____

_____

_____

_____

_____

_____

_____

_____

_____

_____

_____

_____

Name_____ **Date**_____

Do You Like...?

INDIVIDUALS, GROUPS, AND INSTITUTIONS

W Whole-group activity   **S** Small-group activity

I Individual activity   **T** Transition   **RA** Read-aloud

W Talking Without Talking

Explain to children that deaf people cannot hear and many of them cannot speak. Tell them that most deaf people communicate using sign language instead of talking. Show the group a few simple signs and some letters of the alphabet. A good resource for sign-language words is *Signing Illustrated: The Complete Learning Guide* by Mickey Flodin (Perigee, 1994).

W Signing the Alphabet

Spend a few minutes every day teaching children how to sign one or two letters. Use Laura Rankin's *The Handmade Alphabet* (Puffin, 1996) as a resource for children to learn how to form a particular letter without having to ask the teacher.

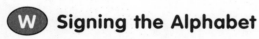

Hello   **A**   **B**   **C**

(S) Puzzle Groups

Invite children to draw an illustration of a special time they shared with a group of people. For example, they might draw themselves participating in a family or neighborhood activity, or playing with school friends on the playground. Have children cut their pictures into four puzzle pieces, and ask a partner to complete the puzzle. Then discuss with children the different groups they belong to, such as their family, class, neighborhood, and so on.

(W) Which Way to Go?

Take children for a quick walk to nearby areas around your classroom, such as the restrooms, cafeteria, office, and the school's front door. Note the directions you took to get to other areas. Back in the classroom, invite children to make signs that point to the different areas in your school, and post them in the hallway outside your classroom.

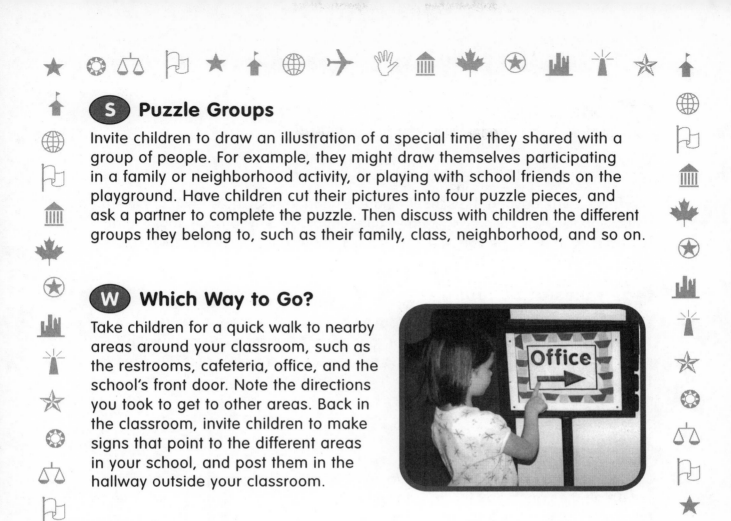

(W) Our Neighborhood

Ask children to note the neighborhood surrounding the school as they come in the morning or leave in the afternoon. Challenge children to use blocks and small manipulatives to recreate different buildings they observed around the neighborhood.

(W) Doing Business

If your school has a nearby shopping area, suggest to children that they pay special attention to it when they visit the area with their families. After a few days of observation time, have children draw pictures of some of the shops to hang in the classroom. Invite the owner of a store or an employee to be a guest speaker in the class. For those children who are not able to go to the shopping area, you can display photographs of the different stores.

RA My Town
by Rebecca Treays (EDC/Usborne, 1998)

Using easy-to-understand text, Treays explains the different components of a community and how a community develops.

Try This! Think beyond the school neighborhood to the whole town or city in which you live. Ask children to identify different places in your town that could be included in all of the components of a community as described in *My Town*.

S Rules at School

Divide the class into groups of four to six children. Ask them to work together for 10 minutes each day for four days, brainstorming and writing rules they follow at school as well as the reason each rule exists. On the fifth day, invite each group to share the rules and the reasons for these rules with the rest of the class.

S Rules at Home

Divide the class into groups of four to six children. Ask them to work together for 10 minutes each day for four days, brainstorming and writing rules they follow at home as well as the reason each rule exists. On the fifth day, invite each group to share the rules and the reasons for these rules with the rest of the class.

I We Do What We've Got to Do

Ask each child to write a list or draw pictures of chores that families have to do (such as laundry, cooking, and shopping) and the person in their family who usually does each task. Ask children to add to the list for three days, then share their list with the whole group. Define the term *role*, and help children make the connection that different family members have different roles within the family group.

I Roles Parents Play

Ask children to choose a parent and draw a picture showing how that person takes care of the home or children. Display the pictures by gender. Compare the pictures of mothers to the pictures of fathers, and talk about how their roles are the same and how they are different.

Ⓘ Speak Into the Microphone, Please

Make microphones from paper-towel holders, still cameras from small boxes, and video cameras from shoe boxes. Keep these items near the meeting area in the classroom. When something noteworthy happens in the class, select a "news crew" to interview the people involved and report to the class.

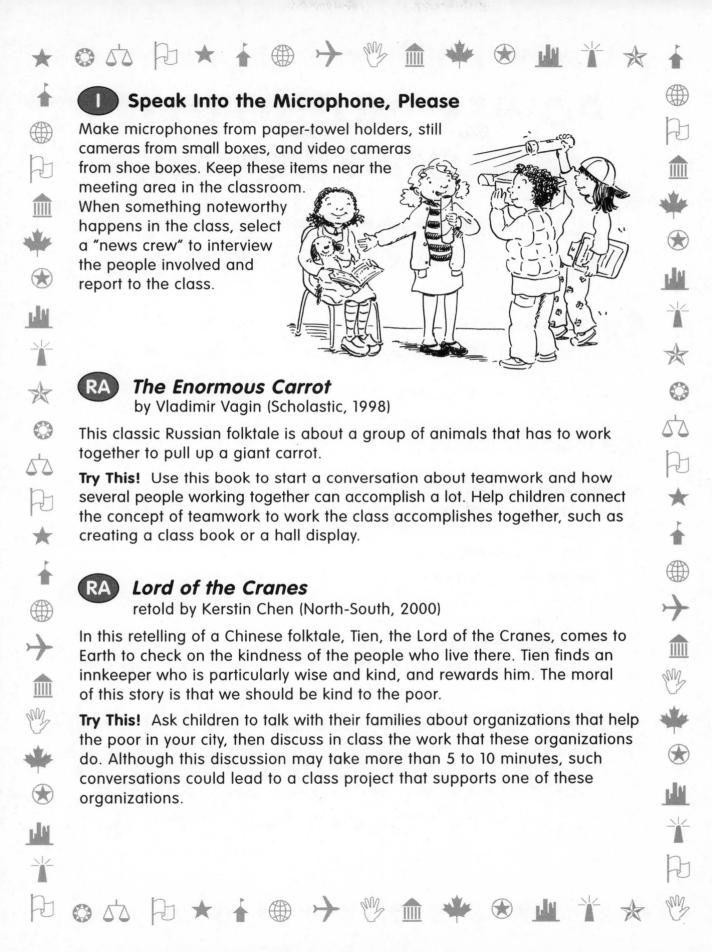

🅡🅐 *The Enormous Carrot*
by Vladimir Vagin (Scholastic, 1998)

This classic Russian folktale is about a group of animals that has to work together to pull up a giant carrot.

Try This! Use this book to start a conversation about teamwork and how several people working together can accomplish a lot. Help children connect the concept of teamwork to work the class accomplishes together, such as creating a class book or a hall display.

🅡🅐 *Lord of the Cranes*
retold by Kerstin Chen (North-South, 2000)

In this retelling of a Chinese folktale, Tien, the Lord of the Cranes, comes to Earth to check on the kindness of the people who live there. Tien finds an innkeeper who is particularly wise and kind, and rewards him. The moral of this story is that we should be kind to the poor.

Try This! Ask children to talk with their families about organizations that help the poor in your city, then discuss in class the work that these organizations do. Although this discussion may take more than 5 to 10 minutes, such conversations could lead to a class project that supports one of these organizations.

POWER, AUTHORITY, AND GOVERNANCE

(W) Whole-group activity　(S) Small-group activity

(I) Individual activity　(T) Transition　(RA) Read-aloud

(W) Our Class Rules

Over several days, hold class meetings that focus on the development of class rules. Lead a discussion about why rules are important and what rules should be established in this particular class.

(W) Logical Consequences

Over several days, present one hypothetical class problem per day and ask children to decide on a fair consequence for child(ren) involved in such a situation. Use some of the following situations to lead these discussions about what is fair:

- Paint is accidentally spilled.
- Homework is forgotten.
- A student refuses to share.
- The page of a library book is torn.
- Caps are left off markers.
- A child forgets to bring lunch to school.

Teaching Tip
Document these class discussions by writing the problems and the solutions on chart paper. You can refer children to this list when one of these situations really happens in the class.

W Rights and Responsibilities

Briefly define the terms *rights* and *responsibilities* at the children's level. Challenge children to list their responsibilities in relation to their rights in different school situations—for example, checking out books from the school library, playing with school equipment during physical education and recess, using community supplies to create paintings or produce books, and so on.

W Who Makes the School Rules?

Invite the principal to talk to the class about why certain rules apply to everyone in the school. Encourage children to ask questions about the people who are involved in creating school rules.

W Majority Rules

Offer two books as options for the next read-aloud. Photocopy the front covers of the books, post them on the chalkboard or on a page from the chart tablet, and draw a line separating the two. Distribute one sticky note per child and pencils or markers. Ask children to write their names on the sticky note and place it under the book that they choose.

Teaching Tip
Young children like voting so much that they often vote for all options when asked to vote by simply raising their hands. To avoid a vote of 30 to 16 in a class with only 25 students, this kind of forced "one person, one vote" method helps children learn how voting really works.

W The Ayes Have It

Introduce the words *aye* and *nay*. Anytime children must make a decision, present the option and have them vote "aye" if they are in favor of it, or "nay" if they are against it.

W For the People, By the People

Discuss the concept of democracy with children. Explain that in other countries, rulers can decide many things that affect other people. But in the United States, we all have a say in what happens through voting, or by writing or phoning our senators and representatives.

RA *The Voices of the People*
by Giulio Maestro (Lothrop Lee & Shepard, 1996)

Targeted for children ages 4 to 8, this book explains the U.S. election process in relatively simple language. Maestro also discusses the responsibilities of the three branches of the federal government and the function of political parties.

Try This! Choose an elected official—the mayor, governor, state or national senator or representative, or the President—for children to write to. Encourage children to ask a question or share an opinion about a current issue.

S Creating a Fair System

Divide the class into groups of four or five children. Using an activity that all children will want to participate in (such as easel painting, caring for class pets, or playing a new game), ask groups to come up with a fair system for deciding which group gets to do the activity first.

① Who Can Tell You What to Do

Ask children to think about people in their lives who can tell them what to do, and have them draw a picture of those people.

The next day, encourage children to share their picture with the whole class and talk about the relationships between children and the people in their lives who can tell them what to do.

RA *Clara Barton, Founder of the American Red Cross*
by Augusta Stevenson (Aladdin, 1986)

This book (from the Childhoods of Famous Americans series) presents Clara Barton's formative years, during which she developed the qualities and characteristics necessary to found the American Red Cross.

Try This! Read this book over several days, discussing with children how a single individual can do such important work and affect his or her community and country the way Clara Barton did.

Try This, Too! Provide the address for the nearest local chapter of the American Red Cross. Ask children to write to the chapter requesting information about this institution that helps so many people.

RA *When They Fight*
by Kathryn White (Winslow, 2000)

Told from the perspective of a young badger who overhears his parents fighting and making up, this book touches on both fear and reassurance. The badger's honesty could be the basis for classroom discussions about family relationships, arguing, and making family decisions.

RA *The Girl Who Wore Too Much*
retold by Margaret Read MacDonald
with Thai text by Supapor Vathanaprida (August House, 1998)

The authors retell this traditional Thai folktale in both English and Thai. The main character of the book, who likes nice clothes and jewelry, learns that it is possible to want too much.

Try This! Use this book as a springboard to a group discussion about a sense of fairness.

PRODUCTION, DISTRIBUTION, AND CONSUMPTION

W Whole-group activity   **S** Small-group activity

I Individual activity   **T** Transition   **RA** Read-aloud

W Natural Resources Word Web

To emphasize things that come from nature, draw a quick nature word web. Write *nature* in the middle, and add words to it as the children name things that are natural, such as water, air, animals, trees, flowers, grass, and sunlight.

S Natural Resources Learning Center

To help reinforce children's understanding of different natural resources, set up a learning center with the web created in the above activity, magazines that feature nature photographs, several posterboards, scissors, and glue sticks. Over several days, encourage children to find and cut out photographs of different natural resources. Ask children to group similar photographs on a posterboard. After children have worked on this activity for several days, use the original web as a model for hanging the posterboards as a huge web.

W Above and Below

Display foods that are grown above ground (such as apples, oranges, okra, cucumbers, and squash) and below ground (potatoes, peanuts, onions, and garlic). Describe food as growing "above" and "below," "over" and "under," and "underground."

W Needs and Wants

On index cards, write several "needs" and "wants." Possible examples include water, bread, shirt, house, computer, video games, trip, toys, and car. Mix up the cards and have a child pick one. Ask children to tell if the word on the card is a "need" or a "want." Place the cards in a pocket chart under the appropriate heading.

W Food Groups

Ask families to save empty containers from food such as yogurt, pasta, vegetables, and rice. Try to get a variety of foods from the different food groups (bread, cereal, rice, and pasta; fruits and vegetables; milk products, cheese, poultry, meat, dried beans, eggs, and fish; and fats, oils, and sweets). Help children sort the containers into the four food groups. Guide them to determine which foods they eat most often and which foods they should eat more often.

W From Tree to Store

Gather a variety of apples and apple products, such as applesauce, apple cider, sliced apples, apple juice, apple pie, and apple jelly. Point out to children how a natural apple can be processed into many products. Give children an opportunity to taste processed apple products and natural apples. (Make sure to check for food allergies first.)

W What Do We Drink?

For a quick taste experiment, gather different juices and small cups. Ask children to sample juices and describe their tastes. (Make sure to check for food allergies first.)

RA *A Busy Day at Mr. Kang's Grocery Store*
by Alice Flanagan (Children's Press, 1997)

Filled with colorful photographs, this book shows what a day is like in the life of a Korean-American storeowner.

Try This! If children have had few personal experiences in grocery stores, the best learning experience would be to take them on a quick field trip to a nearby grocery store.

S Grocery Store

Have children set up their own grocery store in the dramatic-play area of the classroom.

To expand children's vocabulary, enter their play from time to time and purposefully use words such as *checkout*, *aisle*, *shelf*, *shopping cart*, *dairy products*, *produce*, *bakery*, *freezer section*, *grocer*, and *butcher*.

S Grocery Vocabulary

Build basic grocery-store vocabulary—especially for second-language learners—by having children cut out pictures of various foods from magazines and glue them on a posterboard. Help children label the foods and encourage them to play a simple game of "Where Is the _____?"

Teaching Tip
Save the food containers used in the "Food Groups" activity (page 41). Children can use those props when setting up their own grocery store. Add more props to make the grocery store more authentic, such as grocery circulars, a scale, plastic and paper grocery bags, lined paper labeled "Grocery List," and a calculator or two (especially those models that include a paper tape).

(S) Home Center Snack

In the home center, provide a small jar of fruit spread, a variety of breads, a small plastic spreading knife, and small paper plates. Help small groups of children prepare bread and fruit spread sandwiches as part of their pretend play in the home center. (Make sure to check for food allergies first.)

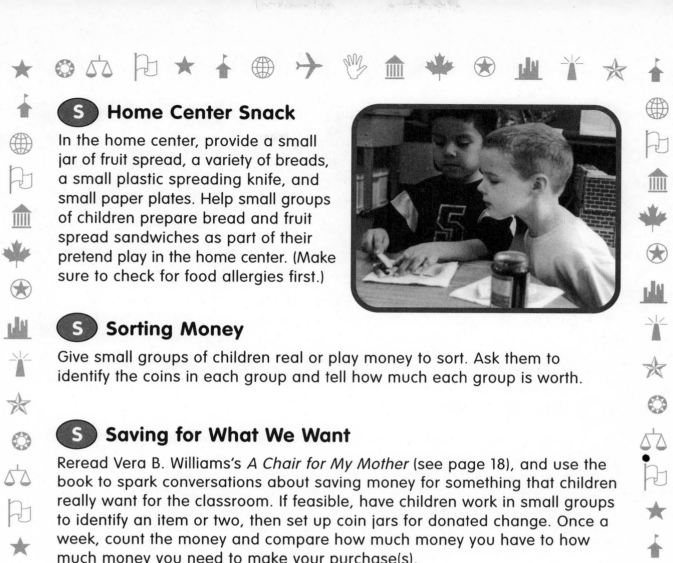

(S) Sorting Money

Give small groups of children real or play money to sort. Ask them to identify the coins in each group and tell how much each group is worth.

(S) Saving for What We Want

Reread Vera B. Williams's *A Chair for My Mother* (see page 18), and use the book to spark conversations about saving money for something that children really want for the classroom. If feasible, have children work in small groups to identify an item or two, then set up coin jars for donated change. Once a week, count the money and compare how much money you have to how much money you need to make your purchase(s).

(S) Money From Around the World

Gather money from other countries. Often international students from a local college can help with this. On a map, match the country with its money. Help children learn the names of money used in other countries.

(S) From the Factory to the Store

Place a large sheet of mural paper on the floor. Label one corner as the factory and the opposite corner as the local store. Encourage children to use blocks to build the factory and the store, then draw train tracks to carry the goods from factory to store.

(S) Train Tracks Game Board

Photocopy the Train Tracks Game Board (pages 46–47) and glue it to the inside of a manila file folder. After children have created the factory-to-store train tracks in the previous activity, invite them to play this game. If possible, provide small train cars for game pieces and dice for children to roll and determine how many spaces they can move on each turn.

(S) Transporting Goods

After children have created the factory-to-store train tracks, add trucks, cars, buses, trains, airplanes, and helicopters to the block area, and boats and barges to the water table. Challenge children to model transporting goods from farms and factories to the stores where people buy the products.

(RA) Literacy Links

Read several books about how food products get from where they are produced to where they are purchased:

- *The Milk Makers* by Gail Gibbons (Aladdin, 1987)
- *Cranberries* by William Jaspherson (Houghton Mifflin, 1991)
- *Apple Farmer Annie* by Monica Wellington (Penguin Putnam, 2001)
- *Market Day* by Lois Ehlert (Harcourt, 2000)
- *Ox-Cart Man* by Donald Hall (Penguin, 1983)

(S) How Can We Get There?

Divide a bulletin board into three sections and label them *Air*, *Land*, and *Water*. Have children look through magazines and cut out pictures of transportation, then place them in the appropriate sections on the bulletin board.

(I) Advertising on Cereal Boxes

Ask parents or other adult volunteers to cover cereal boxes with brown paper. Give each child one cereal box and supply small groups with colored pencils, crayons, markers, paint, and brushes. Challenge children to create a design for their cereal boxes that would attract the attention of other children.

Later in the week, distribute the same supplies to children and challenge them to create a design for their cereal boxes that would attract the attention of adults.

(T) I've Been Working on the Railroad

Sing "I've Been Working on the Railroad" as children march around the classroom or line up to leave for lunch or recess. Adapt the lyrics to other forms of transportation, such as bus, plane, and truck.

(RA) *Eating the Alphabet*
by Lois Ehlert (Harcourt, 1993)

Ehlert paints fruits and vegetables to represent each letter of the alphabet. Many are familiar to young children, but some—including endive, eggplant, kumquat, kiwi, and kohlrabi—will be new to most of them.

Try This! Bring in or ask families to donate unfamiliar fruits and vegetables for children to taste. (Make sure to check for food allergies first.)

Train Tracks
Game Board

Fancy Hat Factory

START

Mountain range! Lose a turn.

Cargo spills! Go back 2 spaces.

Sharp curve! Lose a turn.

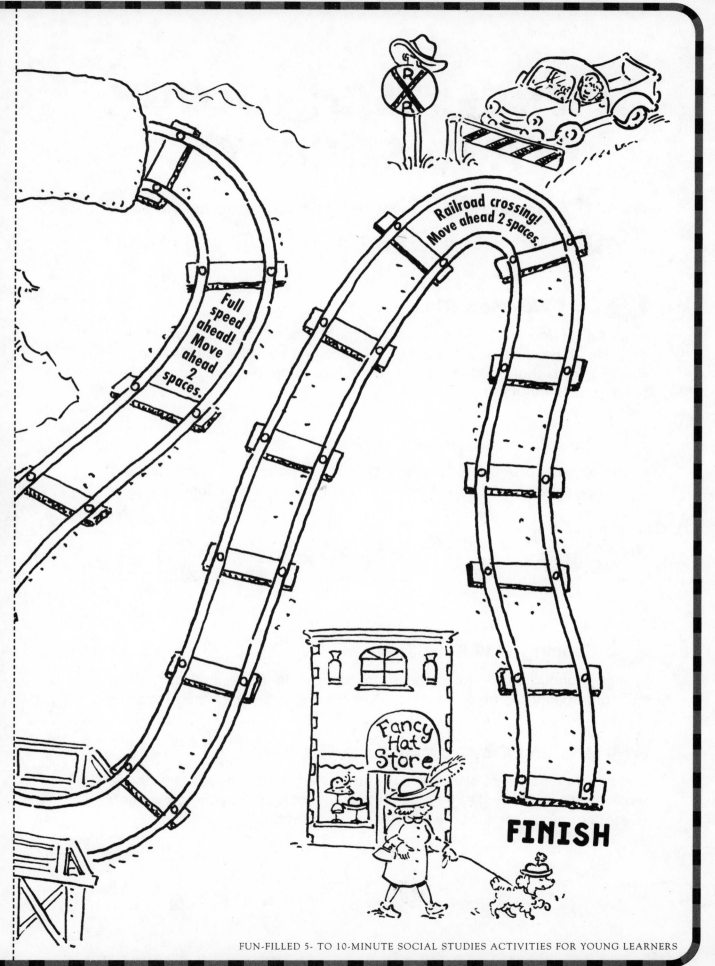

Full speed ahead! Move ahead 2 spaces.

Railroad crossing! Move ahead 2 spaces.

Fancy Hat Store

FINISH

SCIENCE, TECHNOLOGY, AND SOCIETY

W Whole-group activity   **S** Small-group activity

I Individual activity   **T** Transition   **RA** Read-aloud

W Cars Way Back Then

Invite a grandparent or even a great-grandparent to share photographs and talk to the class about cars he or she owned over the years—from Model T Fords that had to be cranked to start, to the modern cars that are familiar to children today.

I Cars Through Time

Photocopy and distribute "Cars Now and Then" (page 51) to each child in the class. Ask children to cut out the cars and put them in chronological order.

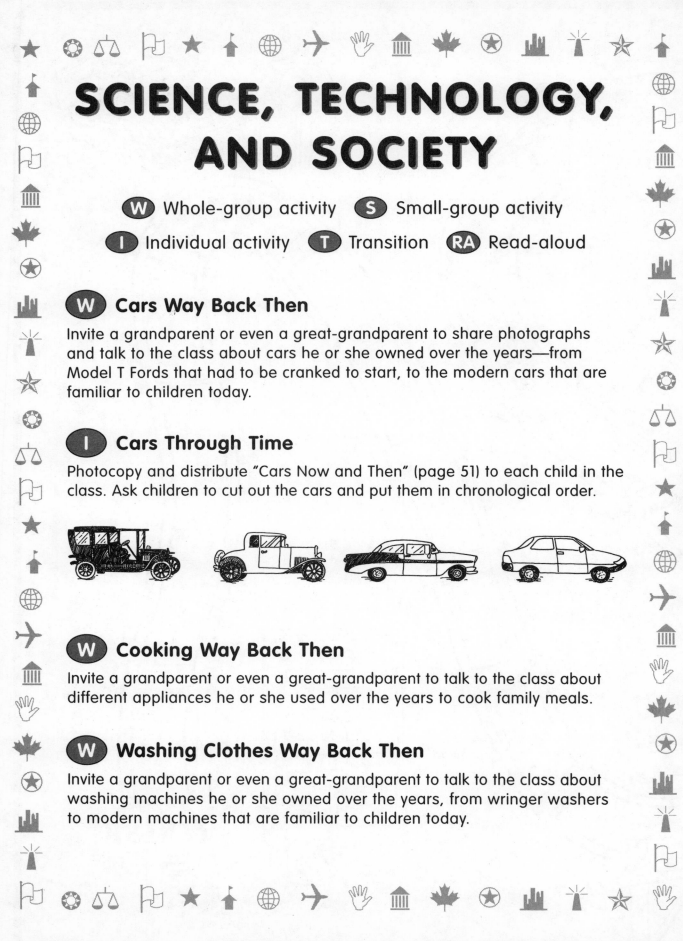

W Cooking Way Back Then

Invite a grandparent or even a great-grandparent to talk to the class about different appliances he or she used over the years to cook family meals.

W Washing Clothes Way Back Then

Invite a grandparent or even a great-grandparent to talk to the class about washing machines he or she owned over the years, from wringer washers to modern machines that are familiar to children today.

S Messages 24/7

Explain to children that cell phones and pagers are relatively recent technologies. Pair up children and assign each pair one adult who works in the school. Have each pair interview their person, asking if he or she had a cell phone or pager when they were in first grade (or whatever grade you are teaching), if they have a cell phone or pager now, and why they use them. When everyone returns to the classroom, have each pair report to the whole group.

S Communicating Now and Then

Divide the class into groups of four to six. Have each group brainstorm a list of different ways they could use technology to communicate with other people. Ask each child to interview an adult in their lives about technology they used as a child to communicate with other people.

On the next day, have groups share information they learned from their interviews. On the third day, graph the number of ways people communicate now and the number of ways they communicated in the past. On the fourth day, compare the graphs.

RA *Taking Flight: The Story of the Wright Brothers*
by Stephen Krensky (Simon & Schuster, 2000)

This is the story of Orville and Wilbur Wright's struggles and successes with their flying machines. Krensky uses short quotations from the Wrights' letters to expand the text.

Try This! Locate a commercial or amateur pilot to talk to the class about the differences between the Wright Brothers' first airplane and a modern plane.

RA *The Real McCoy:*
The Life of an African-American Inventor
by Wendy Towle (Scholastic, 1995)

This book is a biography of Elijah McCoy, made famous by his invention of a special oil cup for trains. McCoy also invented other objects such as rubber heels and lawn sprinklers.

Try This! Follow this read-aloud with a discussion of how our lives today are different because of the inventions of this one man.

RA *The Picture Book of Thomas Alva Edison*
by David A. Adler (Holiday House, 1999)

This biography begins with Edison's quirky childhood and details his long line of inventions.

Try This! List Edison's inventions as you read aloud the book. Discuss about what life today might be like without Edison's inventions.

RA *Next Stop Grand Central*
by Maira Kalman (Putnam/Penguin Putnam, 1999)

The architecture, sights, sounds, and people of New York City's Grand Central Station are depicted in this book, which can prompt conversations about how huge numbers of people in a small area require special forms of transportation.

Try This! If you live in a city with subways or if your students have traveled to cities that have them, ask children to discuss what subways are like and their benefits. If most of the children in your class have never ridden a subway, encourage them to write the Chamber of Commerce in large cities to find out which cities have them.

RA *Mary Anning and the Sea Dragon*
by Jeannine Atkins (Farrar, Straus & Giroux, 1999)

This biography tells the story of Mary Anning (1799–1847) and her constant search for her "curiosities." Anning's curiosities turn out to be *ammonites* (extinct cephalopods, which are related to squids and octopi). The book discusses Anning's special contributions to the field of paleontology.

Cars Now and Then

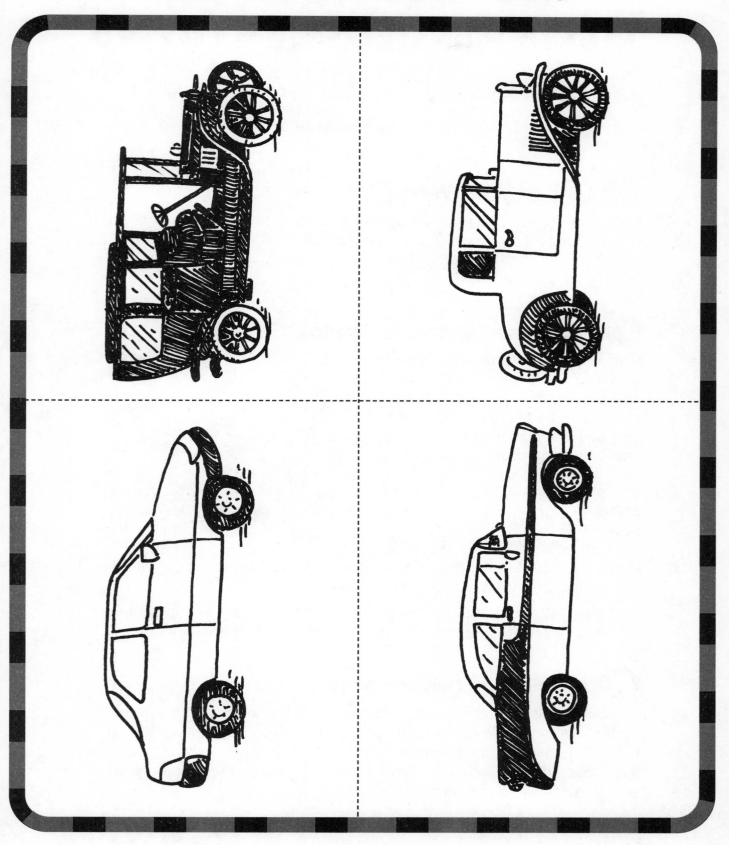

GLOBAL CONNECTIONS

W Whole-group activity **S** Small-group activity
I Individual activity **T** Transition **RA** Read-aloud

W Long May She Wave

Display the American flag for children to see, discussing what the stars and stripes stand for. Invite children to draw a picture of the flag. Then have children draw flags from other countries after researching them, and post the flags around the classroom.

W Music From Around the World

Display musical instruments from around the world. Discuss what the instruments look like and how their sounds are alike and different. Invite children to play an instrument as they listen to music from the country of its origin.

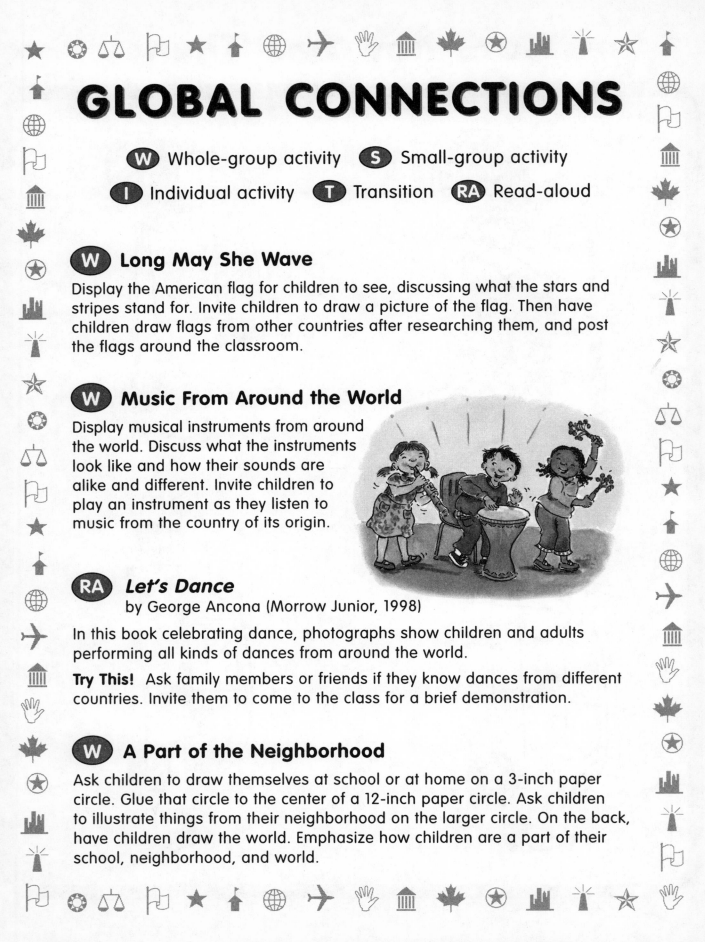

RA *Let's Dance*
by George Ancona (Morrow Junior, 1998)

In this book celebrating dance, photographs show children and adults performing all kinds of dances from around the world.

Try This! Ask family members or friends if they know dances from different countries. Invite them to come to the class for a brief demonstration.

W A Part of the Neighborhood

Ask children to draw themselves at school or at home on a 3-inch paper circle. Glue that circle to the center of a 12-inch paper circle. Ask children to illustrate things from their neighborhood on the larger circle. On the back, have children draw the world. Emphasize how children are a part of their school, neighborhood, and world.